CW00517040

Bobby Brewster's
Jigsaw Puzzle

H. E. Todd

Bobby Brewster's Jigsaw Puzzle

Illustrated by Val Biro

Hodder & Stoughton
LONDON SYDNEY AUCKLAND TORONTO

British Library Cataloguing in Publication Data
Todd, H. E.
    Bobby Brewster's jigsaw puzzle.
    Rn: Balint Stephen Biro   I. Title   II. Biro, Val
    823'.914[J]   PZ7

    ISBN 0-340-42087-1

Text copyright © H. E. Todd 1988
Illustrations copyright © Hodder and Stoughton 1988

First published 1988

Published by Hodder and Stoughton Children's Books,
a division of Hodder and Stoughton Ltd,
Mill Road, Dunton Green, Sevenoaks, Kent TN13 2YJ

Photoset by Rowland Phototypesetting Ltd,
Bury St Edmunds, Suffolk

Printed in Great Britain by St Edmundsbury Press Ltd,
Bury St Edmunds, Suffolk

Contents

Introduction

In the introduction to this book I am happy to thank a number of people.

After a visit to St Luke's C of E School at Lowton in Lancashire Stuart O'Neill sent me a suggestion about a clock. Shortly afterwards I read an interesting letter to the *Sunday Express* from Patricia Williams Burr describing the antics of one of her clocks. So, after getting some facts from Mr De Lisle at his clock-shop in my home town, I wrote 'The Clock Doctor'.

Sara Pilkington, at Huncoat Primary School, Accrington, also in Lancashire, wrote after my visit there about 'The Piece of String', the result of which you can read in this book.

Two stories are based on things that really happened in Berkhamsted, where I live. Dear 'Old Ginger' lived his life exactly as described in my story, and his offspring, Marmaduke and Enid, still are a great comfort to my friend Harry Casserley.

Delightful Daly Stiles, then aged 1½, really did drop his 'Little White Teddy' in Lower Kings Road, and who do you think found it? I did! And I took it home.

Finally I should like to thank everyone at Mount Pleasant Artists' Rest Home in Reigate. I enjoy staying there so much that I am always stimulated to write stories, and three in this book were written during my last stay there.

H. E. TODD
Berkhamsted, February 1987

1　The Jigsaw Puzzle

Do you remember Bobby Brewster's Aunt Angela with the wobbly earrings? I once wrote a story about a remarkable coloured ball that she gave to Bobby as a birthday present. When it was first given to him he thought it was a babyish present for a boy of his age, but – as so often happens with Bobby – it turned out to be magic. It bounced sideways and found things that had been lost, including an earring that Aunt Angela had wobbled off one ear whilst playing hide and seek in the garden. So it was certainly a useful babyish present!

In case you never read that story let me introduce you to Aunt Angela. She is a kind, well-meaning lady who is inclined to be gushing. Her earrings wobble when she speaks and she always carries a large open handbag full of oddments. So

9

she has to fiddle about for a long time whenever she wants to find anything, and then often can't even if it is there! When she arrives on visits she clutches Bobby to her ample bosom, wobbles her earrings at him with a doting expression on her face, and cries, 'Bobby my dear, haven't you grown?' which makes him feel embarrassed. Did she expect him to shrink?

Recently Aunt Angela came on an important visit. She was shortly to go on a trip to Australia to stay with a friend and tour other parts of that country so she was even more excited than usual. And she brought her lady cat, Angelina, with her to leave at the Brewsters, who had rather reluctantly agreed to look after her whilst Aunt Angela was away. Like her mistress, Angelina was lovable but completely scatty! In the garden that cat would slink along the lawn in a menacing way and then suddenly pounce on things that weren't there! In the house she tangled balls of wool with everything in sight and wrapped herself inside paper-bags with loud rustlings. And she had a habit, sometimes annoying, of jumping. She jumped on chairs and tables and she jumped on people without any warning.

But to return to Aunt Angela herself. The present which she brought for Bobby on that visit was sensible for once and quite grown-up.

In fact it was a large jigsaw puzzle. And as Aunt Angela was so excited about her trip to Australia it was not surprising that the complete jigsaw made a picture of a marvellous sight in that country – Ayers Rock.

Have you ever heard of Ayers Rock? I don't think it is one of the Seven Wonders of the World, but it is certainly a marvellous sight. I have never been there myself, but have seen many photographs of it. It is a huge rock a mile and a half long and a bit under a quarter of a mile high, stuck right in the middle of Aborigine country – a remote flat desert of scrub. There it stands, a landmark for miles and, as the sun moves across the sky throughout each day, different colours are reflected on Ayers Rock. It turns from brilliant crimson in the early morning to a magnificent purple at sunset. The Aborigines worship Ayers Rock. It must be truly magical to see.

Not only is the real Ayers Rock magic, but so did that jigsaw puzzle given by Aunt Angela turn out to be – which is perhaps not at all surprising since she gave it to Bobby Brewster, the ordinary boy to whom extraordinary things are always happening.

He took two trays into the sitting-room and, after removing Aunt Angela's bulky handbag and placing it on the sofa, he put them on the table. Then he started to turn out pieces of jigsaw on to one tray so that he could assemble them on the other. At first he did not get on very well, but then a funny thing happened.

A voice from the trays said, 'Find the straight sides and fit them together first.' Bobby was concentrating so hard on his jigsaw puzzle that he followed the advice without thinking where it came from.

Then the same voice said, 'No, you silly boy, blue sky shouldn't be on the ground, even in Australia!'

He then realised that no one else was with him in the sitting-room so he asked, 'Who are you?'

'I'm your jigsaw puzzle,' said the voice.

'Well, you are certainly puzzling to me in more ways than one,' said Bobby.

'Of course I am,' was the reply. 'What's the use of being a jigsaw *puzzle* without being able to puzzle people?'

'That's true, I suppose,' agreed Bobby, 'and since you seem to be magical as well as puzzling perhaps you will help me by offering more advice. Between us we should then be able to piece you together and make a picture of Ayers Rock.'

'Very well, I agree to help you occasionally,'

said the magic puzzle. 'But you must work most of me out for yourself, otherwise I will not be puzzling enough.'

After that Bobby really did get on quite well. Now and then the voice would make helpful remarks like:

'Put all the scrubby-looking pieces together at my base,' or 'Now the purple pieces of Ayers Rock at sunset.'

The puzzle began to take shape, and Bobby was excited and proud of himself.

Then came disaster! Unbeknown to Bobby, Angelina the cat had crept into the sitting-room. She made one of her sudden jumps on to the table and landed – PLONK! – right into the middle of the

half-finished jigsaw puzzle. All the pieces from both trays flew over the floor in different directions. They shot under the bureau and they shot out of the door into the hall. Some jumped on to the bureau and sofa and some even managed to jump out of open windows!

'*Angelina!*' yelled Bobby, and his parents, with Aunt Angela, ran into the sitting-room to find him almost in tears.

'Oh dear, what a mess!' they said – and Aunt Angela wobbled her earrings and cried, 'Angelina, you naughty, naughty cat!'

Then they all got on hands and knees to search for the scattered pieces of jigsaw. This took a long time, and, whilst they were still at it, Aunt Angela had to say her farewells. And it really *was* farewell, because she would be off on her tour of Australia in a few days and would not see them again until she returned home months later.

Well, after she had left, most of the missing pieces of jigsaw were found, but for several days little bits turned up in unlikely places. One morning, when her vacuum-cleaner started making protesting noises, Mrs Brewster found that she had even sucked some of the pieces up!

As you can imagine, Bobby was discouraged after the tragedy. He felt almost inclined to throw the puzzle away, but then thought it would seem ungrateful to Aunt Angela, who might enquire about it when she next came on a visit. So he left it in his bedroom and forgot all about it.

Then, one evening at bedtime, he heard that voice again. It said, 'What about *me*?'

He knew what was talking but still felt discouraged so he replied, 'Well, *what* about you?'

'Isn't it time you tried to fit me together again?' said the puzzle.

'Oh, all right, I will have a go at you tomorrow,' Bobby grudgingly agreed. 'As long as you promise to help me.'

'I will help you on one condition,' said the puzzle. 'You *must* keep that cat out of the way.'

On the following day Bobby put the two trays on his bed and then firmly shut the door to keep Angelina out. And this time he and the jigsaw puzzle got on really well together. Not only did the puzzle offer useful advice but once or twice it even fitted *itself* together before Bobby's eyes. It was a most surprising sight.

There was, however, more disappointment to come. When all the pieces were used up they formed into a picture with a hole in the middle. And a hole in a vital point – most of Ayers Rock was missing! And what is the good of a picture of Ayers Rock without Ayers Rock? Bobby was

bitterly disappointed. Where could those missing pieces of jigsaw possibly have gone?

You will never guess the answer. I certainly
didn't until Bobby told me what had happened
later. Several letters arrived from Aunt Angela,
telling them about her travels in Australia. Then,
in one rather bulky letter, she described her trip
to Aborigine country to see Ayers Rock. This is
what she wrote: 'We were there at sunset and it
was a magnificent sight – a giant block of vivid
purple that completely dominated the landscape.
It was magic!' Then she added, 'And after we
returned to the hotel another magic thing happened. I was searching in my handbag and what
do you think I found? Some pieces of Bobby's
jigsaw puzzle! They must have fallen into my
open handbag that afternoon when Angelina
jumped on the trays. I am sure that Bobby is
missing them, so here they are.'

And there they certainly were, in the envelope
with Aunt Angela's letter.

But, even more amazing, when Bobby fitted
them in to complete the jigsaw puzzle Ayers
Rock was a far more vivid purple than in the
picture on the lid of the box. So those pieces sent
back from Australia must have changed into
true-life colours after seeing the real thing!

There is only one logical explanation. That

magic talking jigsaw puzzle had been dissatisfied with itself when it was first made. And the most important pieces – those of Ayers Rock – had deliberately arranged to travel with Aunt Angela to Australia to find out what they really should look like. Then they had made sure that Aunt Angela posted them home to Bobby so that he could complete the puzzle with Ayers Rock complete in true colours.

Now that so many people say what a beautiful

picture the jigsaw has made Bobby has never separated the pieces again. He keeps it intact in a box with the lid open for everyone to admire. And it is so proud of itself that at bedtime, when they are alone, it often tells Bobby exciting Aborigine folk tales!

Which proves beyond all doubt that it is a truly magic jigsaw puzzle, doesn't it?

2 The Clock Doctor

Clocks are like people. For one thing they all have a face. And there are many different kinds of clock face just as people have different faces. Then there are boy and girl clocks, gentlemen and lady clocks, and grandfather and grandmother clocks. Each has a different chime – happy – ladylike – booming – sometimes almost apologetic!

I am sure that clocks can talk to each other too. To us it may only sound like ticking, but think of how many different kinds of tick there are. After all, people talk to each other with different voices in different languages. Birds twitter to each other with different twitters – so why shouldn't clocks tick to each other from one room to another with different ticks? Like this . . .

Kitchen clock (female voice): 'Tick very tick

cold tick today tick, isn't tick it tick?'

(I will leave out the ticks for the rest of this conversation because they make tedious reading. So you must imagine them for yourself.)

Hall clock (male voice): 'Yes, I'm glad they've put the central heating on.'

Kitchen clock: 'How's your cold today?'

Hall clock: 'My chime's a bit hoarse but it's getting better, thank you.'

Now in the Brewster house there are two clocks that are particular friends of the family. Of course there are other clocks as well – all useful – but those two clocks are a special part of the household.

Firstly, there's the alarm clock in Bobby's bedroom. It has a cheerful baby face with a wide smile – and honest-to-goodness ordinary hour numbers. But, though it remains as happy as a child, it is by no means young. In fact it was bought in a sale, before the present currency, for 9/11¾d. (That would be about 50p today.) It has a jolly tick that soothes Bobby to sleep at bed-time and wakes him up happy in the morning. It has never gone wrong, even after being dropped on the floor and bouncing – which I regret to say has happened several times. And it has a loud alarm that not only wakes Bobby in his adjacent bed, but also his mother and father in their bedroom and all the other clocks in the house as well. And when they hear the alarm they all say to each other, 'There goes Charley, dead on time as usual.'

Yes, I forgot to tell you before, his name really is Charley. Bobby Brewster gave it to him because he always makes Bobby laugh like he does at the old Charlie Chaplin films on the television. So from now on in this story he will be called Charley and be a 'he' instead of an 'it'.

The other family clock really *is* a family clock because it has come down through the family from Great Grandfather Henry Brewster. It is a solid square no-nonsense mantelpiece clock with roman numerals, and on its back is a brass plate engraved with these words:

Presented to Henry Brewster Esq.
on his retirement
by his many colleagues and friends,
1st January 1891.

It has a deep masculine chime and a sensible regular tick and looks as if it ought to belong to a bank manager, which is not surprising because that is exactly what Henry Brewster Esq. was when he was alive and working. And, of course, a bank manager's clock would never go wrong, would it? And Henry, which naturally is his name, is also obviously a 'he' and not an 'it'.

Did I say that Henry never went wrong? Well, *I* was wrong. After all the years since 1891 when he had kept perfect time, a few weeks ago he started to lose and his tick, instead of being regular, behaved oddly and missed beats. As for his chime, instead of being deep and masculine it began to sound cracked.

The Brewsters took Henry to Mr De Lisle, who keeps the local clock-shop, and left him there for a day or two. But when Mr De Lisle returned Henry he said that to be honest he had not been able to find anything wrong with him and had merely adjusted his timing.

But then, after two days back on his dining-room mantelpiece, Henry started ailing again, losing time and chiming in a cracked voice.

Then Bobby Brewster had an idea. Charley, my alarm clock, always keeps me cheerful, he thought. I wonder if he might cheer up Henry?

So, after being wakened by Charley's happy alarm the following morning, he took him downstairs and put him on the mantelpiece, right next door to poor old Henry.

Henry gained a little time – but not enough. And his chime became clearer – but not clear enough, and that was a step in the right direction.

Then, when Bobby was all by himself in the dining-room, Charley began to sing instead of tick. He did, really. And this is what he sang, to the tune of 'Boys and girls come out to play':

> 'Cheer up, Henry, don't be sick.
> It's very bad to be losing time.
> Give yourself a regular tick
> And put a chuckle in your chime.'

And it worked! Henry immediately perked up. He kept perfect time again and chimed with a deep masculine chuckle chime. And he has done so ever since. But of course Bobby realised that Charley only sang his magic song when no other people but himself were about.

The next clock trouble in the Brewster house came from Katie, the kitchen wall-clock, who began to wheeze. Perhaps all those cooking smells had got into her works. Charley soon dealt with her trouble.

Bobby put him on the shelf nearest to her and, when his mother and father were out, he heard Charley singing, again to the tune of 'Boys and girls come out to play':

'Cheer up, Katie, all is well,
Have no more fears of going slow,
When air is full of cooking smell,
Just give your nose an explosive blow!'

And it worked again! There was an explosive noise from Katie, which must have been her nose being blown, and all was well. And from time to time, from then onwards, after a long kitchen cooking session and when Mrs Brewster is not in, Katie blows her nose and clears all the kitchen smells from her works, and there are no more signs of wheezing or slowness.

Then, one day when in the town shopping,

Bobby called into Mr De Lisle's shop to tell him that Henry had been completely cured through being cheered up by Charley and that the same cure had worked on their kitchen clock as well. Mr De Lisle had never heard anything like it before in the whole of his clock-mending career, and I'm not surprised, are you?

'I wish he would cheer up one of my present patients,' said Mr De Lisle. 'Someone has brought in a cuckoo-clock that persists in going backwards. The cuckoo even sings backwards; instead of singing 'Cuck-oo' it sings 'Oo-cuck!'

'If you like I will bring Charley in and get him to try,' offered Bobby. 'But you will have to put me in a room alone with Charley and the

cuckoo-clock because Charley doesn't like other people seeing him at work.'

Mr De Lisle had never heard anything like that before either, but he said that he was willing to try anything. So that afternoon Bobby took Charley to Mr De Lisle, who put them in a room at the back of the shop, all alone with the cuckoo-clock. This showed the time as five past nine in the morning although it was really twenty-five to three in the afternoon. Then, when the hands of the cuckoo-clock moved backwards to nine o'clock, out came the cuckoo on to the balcony and sang 'Oo-cuck' four times for the hour, and then proceeded to 'Oo-cuck' nine more times for the time.

By then Charley's baby face was looking more worried than cheerful, but he must have had an idea because he stopped ticking and started to sing instead:

'Mice blind three, mice blind three' – which was 'Three Blind Mice' backwards, both words and tune!

Just before its hands moved backward to a quarter to nine the cuckoo came out and stood on the balcony listening with a puzzled expression. Then Charley went on with his backwards song:

'Run they how see, run they how see.'

By then the cuckoo-clock hands showed a

quarter to nine, but this time, instead of singing 'Oo-cuck' three times for the quarter to, it
merely sang 'Oo – oo – oo' without any 'Cucks',
and then waited on the balcony to hear what was
going to happen next.

Charley evidently thought that he must be on
the right track because he continued with his
backwards song, slowly and deliberately:

'Wife farmer's the after ran all they . . .' There
was a pause and the cuckoo looked worried, so
the song continued:

'Knife carving a with tails their off cut she . . .'
The cuckoo looked even more worried . . .
another pause . . . then from Charley:

'Life your in thing a such see you ever did . . .'

By then the hands of the cuckoo-clock showed
half past eight and as Charley concluded his
backwards song with: 'Mice blind three as,' the
cuckoo sang in a clear voice, 'Cuck-oo, cuck-oo,'
to denote the half hour – and with a look of great
relief.

What is more, five minutes later the hands of
that cuckoo-clock had moved forwards to five
and twenty to nine, so all was well again! Charley had proved to that cuckoo-clock that moving
hands and singing backwards made no sense and
was a waste of time. And from that day to this
the cuckoo-clock has never acted so silly again.

Bobby moved its hands forwards to a quarter past three (which if you work it out carefully, you will find was the correct time by then) and went and told Mr De Lisle that the cure was complete.

But he never told Mr De Lisle *how* the cure had been completed because he wanted to keep Charley's real magic all to himself. And even if he had told Mr De Lisle, I doubt if he would have been believed, don't you?

Well, as you can imagine, the Brewster household is now completely free of clock trouble, and should any occur in the future baby-faced Charley – who is far more clever than he looks – will always be there to deal with it. And Mr De Lisle is happy to know that Bobby is always willing to bring Charley along in an emergency. Not that there is likely to be one. Mr De Lisle is a clever clock-mender who can deal efficiently with all normal clock trouble. He is only at a loss with exceptional patients like cuckoo-clocks that move backwards and sing 'Oo-cuck' and I don't blame him, do you?

3   *The Little White Teddy*

It was twelve days before Christmas and Bobby Brewster and his father were on their way home from Christmas shopping in the town. There had been rain and the pavements were wet.

Then, passing down Lower Kings Road, Bobby noticed a bit of fluff in a puddle. He walked on a few paces and something made him turn back to look more closely. What a good thing he did, both for him and the bit of white fluff! Do you know what it turned out to be?

A little white teddy-bear, lying in the gutter with his face in a muddy puddle.

Bobby picked him up, and very dirty and bedraggled he looked, with his red tongue hanging out and a wet black nose. Mr Brewster quickly lifted him to his lips and, in spite of the mud, gave him the kiss of life – just in time!

Slowly little white Teddy recovered and opened his eyes, but he was sopping wet all over and shivering with cold. Bobby wrapped him up gently in his handkerchief before putting him into his warm pocket, and they hurried home.

'Poor little white Teddy!' cried Mrs Brewster when she saw him. She immediately carried him upstairs and gave him a lovely warm bath in the bathroom hand-basin. Then she laid him carefully against a warm pipe and left him there to sleep whilst she and Bobby closed the bathroom door and tiptoed downstairs.

Of course Bobby was anxious to know all the time how little white Teddy was getting on, but his mother told him to be patient and stay very quiet to allow him to sleep. Then, when Bobby was allowed to return upstairs two hours later, there was little white Teddy, spotlessly clean and perky, with the tip of his red tongue still hanging out and a cheeky smile on his face. And, as soon as he saw Bobby, do you know what he did? He winked – a great big wink with the left eye. So of course Bobby winked back.

And what a delightful little chap he turned out to be! In no time the whole Brewster family loved him. At bedtime Bobby took him upstairs and they spent the whole night snuggling together in bed. Then in the morning little white Teddy would wake up looking perkier than ever. And the first thing he always did was to wink at Bobby – a great big wink with the left eye – so of course Bobby winked back.

But, although he settled so well into the Brewster family, they had to realise that he really belonged to someone else and, especially with Christmas approaching, that someone would be missing him sorely. Bobby and his father composed a letter, and sent a copy to each of the three local papers. This is what it said:

Dear Mr Editor,

On the morning of December 13th I found, lying with his face in a puddle in the gutter of Lower Kings Road, a delightful little white teddy-bear, with a black nose and a red tongue hanging out. He was given the kiss of life by my father and a nice hot bath by my mother and has now completely recovered. He is happy and quite at home with us but of course would like to spend Christmas in his own home, so if the owner will call at this house I will gladly hand him over.

Yours hopefully,
Bobby Brewster

and his address.

Bobby didn't really mean the 'gladly' bit about handing him over and was not truly hopeful that little white Teddy would be claimed, but he knew in his heart of hearts that he should return to where he belonged.

It was several days before the local papers were published and the Brewsters became more and more attached to little white Teddy. All day he would settle on the sitting-room sideboard with a happy smile on his face and whenever they were there alone together he and Bobby would exchange great big winks with the left eye. But one night, after returning home late from a party, Bobby and his parents were so tired that Bobby forgot and went upstairs to bed without him. In the middle of the night Mrs Brewster shook her husband (who was snoring) and whispered urgently, 'Listen – I'm sure there's someone downstairs.'

They strained to hear and, yes, there was no doubt about it, something was happening in the sitting-room. Mr Brewster bravely tiptoed down the stairs and opened the sitting-room door softly, carrying a stick aloft ready to strike in case he was attacked.

What do you think he saw? Poor little white Teddy sobbing his heart out because he had been forgotten. So that was the noise that had wakened Mrs Brewster!

Mr Brewster tucked him up in his pyjama

pocket and for the rest of the night he was cuddled to sleep by Bobby's mother. He woke in the morning perkier than ever. But little white Teddy didn't wink at Mrs Brewster – not even with his right eye – because it is rude to wink at ladies without being encouraged to do so.

A few days after Bobby's letter was published in the local papers the telephone rang. On the other end was a lady saying that she thought that little white Teddy belonged to her son. Arrangements were made for them to call and that very evening she arrived with a delightful little boy called Daly Stiles, who was one and a half.

Daly had with him another little teddy-bear with a black nose and sticking-out red tongue. He looked just like little white Teddy except that he was honey-coloured instead of white.

Immediately they entered the sitting-room it was obvious that little white Teddy recognised them. He was handed to Daly, who clutched his two teddies together in his arms and they had a touching reunion – all three of them.

Daly's mother explained that, although they looked alike, they were not twin teddies. Little white Teddy came from Switzerland and little honey Teddy was a local bear. They had been given to Daly by two different people and they had become inseparable friends. So of course little honey Teddy had been grieving ever since his friend disappeared.

There were tears in Bobby's eyes when Daly and his mother took the bears away, and even the eyes of his mother and father glistened more than usual. But it was a happy reunion for little white Teddy, wasn't it? And as he was being carried away, do you know what he did? He looked straight at Bobby and winked – a great big wink with the left eye – so of course Bobby winked back. But no one else noticed them.

During the following few days, when out shopping in the town, the Brewsters were asked by so many people who had read Bobby's letter about little white Teddy that he and his father composed a second letter, which was duly published. It told everyone who was interested that little white Teddy had been returned to his own family, and the Brewsters were frequently told how pleased people were that the story had such a happy ending.

In fact it was not quite the end. This story has to be full of letters, I'm afraid. On Christmas Eve Bobby received a Christmas card with yet another letter enclosed:

Dear Bobby,
Thank you for finding my little white

Teddy and taking such good care of him whilst he was staying with you. He is very pleased to be home, but I think he misses you all because you were so kind and he was rather looking forward to sitting on your Christmas tree. Instead we have hung him on our Christmas tree next to his friend, little honey Teddy, and they both look very pleased with themselves. Once Christmas is over I am going to hang them together on the end of my cot, which will stop little white Teddy from going off on any more adventures without me.

Happy Christmas and love from
Daly

Wasn't that a beautifully expressed letter from a one and a half year old?

Since then Bobby has called at Daly's home several times, and there is no doubt that little white Teddy recognises him at once. You can guess what he does, can't you? He looks straight at Bobby and winks – a great big wink with the left eye – so of course Bobby winks back. But it is always a secret wink just between the two of them, because no one else ever takes any notice.

4   *The Golden Eagle*

When Bobby Brewster was quite a small boy he went to St Peter's Sunday School regularly. He enjoyed it, too, because they told him such lovely stories. Sometimes he himself drew lovely pictures, and they all joined together in singing lovely hymns. Towards the end of each Sunday morning service the Sunday School children walked into church. And what a lovely old church it is!

One morning Bobby's mother heard him singing one of the lovely hymns to himself at home. She asked him whether he would like to join the choir and he said 'Yes'.

To become a member of the choir he had to file up with the other newcomers to the altar, where the vicar laid his hands on their heads and blessed them one by one. It was all very impressive.

The choir was great fun. When Bobby was promoted to wearing a white surplice and a white ruff round his neck his mother thought he looked angelic, though she knew that sometimes he was far from being an angel. They learned beautiful music which they sang with gusto. The only difficult times were when Bobby and his choirboy friends got the giggles during sermons. This happened once when a pigeon flew round and round during the most serious bits and the giggles were almost impossible to stifle. Then, of course, there were the summer choir outings when they always had plenty to eat. Last year they had ices and sardine sandwiches.

Now, each Sunday the lessons at services were read by different people in the congregation, and sometimes members of the choir were selected for this duty. On his way out of church recently Bobby was asked by a Church Warden to read the lesson in a fortnight's time and given details so he could read it beforehand. He was, of course, flattered, but at the same time butterflies started fluttering in his tummy. Standing up all by himself in front of all those people would be quite an ordeal.

And the butterflies in Bobby's tummy were not the only things that fluttered during the next few days, as you find out if you read to the end of this story – which I hope you will!

On his way home from school during the following week Bobby was passing St Peter's Church when he had an idea. He slipped inside the church, made sure that no one was about, and decided to rehearse his lesson out loud. He had his Bible in his satchel with a bookmark at the right page, and he went up two steps to the lectern, which was a large shining brass eagle with outstretched wings. Lots of churches have lecterns like that. Very likely yours has. He opened his Bible at the Book of Daniel chapter three, put it on the outstretched wings of the eagle, and started to read at verse seventeen. He had to stand on tiptoe to see.

His lesson included three people with unusual names, and when he reached their names he declaimed loudly:

'Shadrach, Meshach, and Abendigo.'

Then a very funny thing happened. A voice said, 'No, not Abendigo, Abedngio'.

'I beg your pardon?' said Bobby Brewster.

'The name is ABEDNIGO, with the D *before* the N, not after it,' explained the voice.

But there was nobody in the church. Who on earth could it be? Bobby didn't even have to ask, because the voice added, 'It's me, the golden eagle speaking, and my name is George. I've heard so many lessons read in my time that I know most of them by heart.'

'Goodness gracious me!' exclaimed Bobby.

'And I'll tell you something else,' continued George the golden eagle. 'I can arrange how well or how badly each lesson is read. It depends on whether I approve of the reader or not. You wait till next Sunday. Mr Bompass is going to perform, and he's a proper old hypocrite.'

'What's a hypocrite?' asked Bobby.

'Someone who comes to church regularly and doesn't really mean it,' explained George. 'And next Sunday I will cook old Bompass's goose for him properly.'

'Fancy an eagle cooking a goose,' said Bobby – but it wasn't a very funny joke so George made no comment.

When the following Sunday came Mr Bompass stalked up to the lectern, trying to look impressive. You will meet Mr Bompass in another story. He is the only person in the district who Bobby and his parents really dislike. He manages to be both bumptious and pompous at the same time, so Bompass is the right name for him.

First, when he stood at the golden eagle lectern, Mr Bompass importantly announced the book, chapter, and verse of his lesson, details of which he had memorised. But when he looked downwards someone had turned over the pages of the Bible. I wonder who? Your guess is as good as mine, and probably exactly the same! The result was that Mr Bompass had to search

for the proper place and became flustered before he could even start reading. And then his throat started tickling and he had a coughing fit. But worse was to come. At the vital part he hurriedly pulled a handkerchief from his pocket and let out an explosive 'ATISHOO!'

You can guess the state of Bobby Brewster and his choirboy friends by then, can't you? Even the rest of the congregation – including the vicar – had difficulty in keeping straight faces.

On the following Thursday afternoon Bobby popped into church all by himself again and walked up to the lectern.

'I told you I would cook old Bompass's goose for him, didn't I?' said George the golden eagle.

'You did, and you most certainly kept your promise,' agreed Bobby. 'You cooked it to a turn!'

'Yes, and next Sunday is *your* turn,' said George. 'But I won't lose *your* place or give *you* a coughing and sneezing fit.'

'Good,' said Bobby most relieved.

'Now just have another little run through,' continued George, 'and I will give you some tips to polish up your delivery.'

Bobby rehearsed his lesson. He stuttered a bit with the 'Abednigo' at first, but got it right in the end.

'Not half bad,' encouraged George. 'But you still need a little more confidence. I'll tell you what I will do. Between now and Sunday there are no services so I will take the opportunity of flying off for a few days. Don't worry – I will return for Sunday service in good time so refreshed that I will be able to help you read your lesson expertly.'

And to Bobby's amazement George the golden eagle took off, flew a few trial circuits round the church, and swooped out of the main door!

On his way home Bobby thought that he must have been dreaming, but on the following day, when he peeped inside the church, the lectern steps were there, but no sign of George the golden eagle. Before Sunday luckily neither the vicar, the verger, nor the church-wardens noticed his absence. And the lady who cleans all the brass was on holiday – like George – so she was not there to miss him.

But a lot of people in the area *did* see George, particularly the birdwatchers. He made quite a sensation. There was a headline in the local paper – REMARKABLE BIRD SEEN ON TOP OF CHURCH STEEPLE, with a long, excited article about it. Even the national press published reports of the sighting of the first golden eagle to be seen in the

South of England for over a century. But no one
– except Bobby Brewster – ever suspected that
it was the golden eagle from inside St Peter's
church. The usual explanation was that it must
have lost its way and flown down from the
Highlands of Scotland.

Bobby looked inside the church on the

following Saturday afternoon and was worried to see no sign of the golden eagle. But, even as he was looking, there was a loud swishing noise and through the main doorway swooped George, landing perfectly behind the steps going up to the lectern. He was out of breath at first but then he gasped, 'I've had the time of my life, and tomorrow I shall be so full of beans that your reading of the lesson will amaze the whole congregation.'

And it most certainly did. That Sunday morning lesson about Shadrach, Meshach and – wait for it – ABEDNIGO was declaimed by Bobby in such ringing tones (especially the bit about the burning fiery furnace) that, when he finished, his friends in the choir and the whole congregation, lead by the vicar, burst into a spontaneous round of applause loud enough to rattle the rafters of the grand old church. Which was something that had never happened before at the end of a lesson and is unlikely ever to happen again.

And, whilst Bobby stood speechless at his reception, he distinctly heard through all the noise a whisper from George the golden eagle, 'I told you so!'

5   Up the Wall

One morning Bobby Brewster was lying in bed, when he saw a fly walking up the wall, and across the ceiling, upside down, without going bonk on its head. Bobby Brewster watched it for a little while, and then he said to himself, 'I wish that fly would teach me how to walk up the wall, and across the ceiling, upside down, without going bonk on my head.' At least, he thought he said it to himself but he can't have done, because a very funny thing happened. The fly answered him. It did, really.

'I couldn't do that,' said the fly.

Of course, Bobby Brewster was very surprised at hearing the fly talk at all.

'Well, if you are clever enough to speak,' said Bobby Brewster, 'surely you're clever enough to teach me how to walk up the wall and across the ceiling, upside down, without going bonk on my head?'

'I may be clever enough,' said the fly, 'but my friends would never let me. You see, it isn't much fun being a fly, but one of the few advantages is that you can walk up the wall, and across the ceiling, upside down, without going bonk on your head. If I told you how to do it, it wouldn't be a fly secret, would it?'

'No, I suppose not,' said Bobby Brewster, 'but it's a pity all the same.'

The fly went on walking up the wall, and then suddenly it stopped.

'I tell you what,' said the fly, 'I'll make a bargain with you.'

'I don't know what a bargain is,' said Bobby Brewster.

'Well,' said the fly, 'if you will leave a nice feast for me and my friends out in the garden tonight, I'll come here again tomorrow morning, and I'll teach you how to walk up the wall, and across the ceiling, upside down, without going bonk on your head.'

'Of course, I will,' said Bobby Brewster. 'What would you like to eat?'

'Sardine sandwiches,' said the fly.

Bobby Brewster was very excited the next day, although he tried not to show it. During the afternoon he tried to be very good, and sure enough, just before tea, his mother asked him what he would like to eat, so, of course, he asked for sardines. He was careful to leave one sandwich, and when tea was cleared up he quietly took it outside and put it on the ledge in the garden. He went to bed very early that night, and his mother said, 'Bobby, I *am* surprised. You don't usually want to go to bed as early as this.'

You may be surprised now, thought Bobby Brewster, but just wait till tomorrow morning. You'll be even more surprised when you see me walking up the wall, and across the ceiling, upside down, without going bonk on my head. So he closed his eyes and went to sleep.

There was great activity in the garden that night, though nobody heard anything, because it was only flies. Bobby's fly and all its friends went to the ledge in the garden, and found to their delight that he had remembered about the sardine, so they all started to eat. Now, if there is one thing that Bobby's fly likes more than another it is sardines. It ate so much that at twelve o'clock it was twice as fat as it had been at ten, and by five o'clock the next morning it was twice as fat as it had been at midnight, so you can imagine how big it looked. Then it suddenly thought, Oh, dear! I've got to fly up to Bobby

48

Brewster's room and teach him how to walk up the wall, and across the ceiling, upside down, without going bonk on his head.

It was just as well the fly started to go upstairs early, because it found it very difficult to fly. It had to stop at every step to get more breath, and by the time it got into Bobby Brewster's bedroom and was standing on the top of the brass knob on his bedstead, it was puffing so loudly that it woke Bobby Brewster up.

'Hullo, fly,' said Bobby. 'You don't look very well this morning!'

'I don't feel very well,' said the fly. 'I've eaten too much sardine sandwich.'

'I thought you looked a bit peculiar,' said Bobby Brewster. 'Don't forget you promised to teach me how to walk up the wall, and across the ceiling, upside down, without going bonk on my head.'

'I hadn't forgotten,' said the fly. 'That's what I'm here for. Now, I'll tell you what. First of all, I'll show you how it's done, then I'll explain it, and then *you* can try.'

'That sounds like a good idea,' said Bobby Brewster.

Well, the fly started to walk up the wall, but it took much longer than usual because it was so full of sardine. When it got to the ceiling, it turned upside down and went on walking – one step, two steps, three steps, and then, BONK, it fell on its head.

As the fly staggered to its feet Bobby jumped out of bed and asked anxiously, 'Are you all right, fly?'

But when that poor fly fell it hit its head so hard that from that day to this it has never been able to talk again.

So I'm very sorry to have to tell you that Bobby Brewster *still* doesn't know how to walk up the wall, across the ceiling, upside down without going BONK on his head.

Isn't that a pity?

6 *The Piece of String*

It first arrived for Bobby Brewster by post, tied round a birthday present from his cousin Barbara. And the funny thing was that, though the present itself was exciting enough, the piece of string used to tie round the parcel turned out to be even more exciting!

It was dazzling white string and a long piece, because Barbara had wrapped the parcel securely to make sure that it would not come undone in the post by tying the string round and round and round. And it was secured with such a tight knot that Bobby, who had recently had his fingernails cut – they were clean for once! – could not untie it. So he fetched a pair of scissors. Then the first funny thing happened.

'Please don't cut me,' cried a voice.

'I beg your pardon?' said Bobby Brewster.

'Please don't cut me,' repeated the voice.

'Who *are* you?' asked Bobby Brewster.

'I'm the piece of string,' was the reply, 'and I'm magic.'

'You must be if you can talk,' said Bobby. 'But what's the use of being magic if I can't untie your knot?'

'Very well, I will *prove* how magic I am by making my knot fall apart,' said the string.

Which it promptly did.

'Now you know I'm magic,' continued the

string, 'and may I advise you always to keep me in your pocket so that I can show how useful my magic can be when each occasion arises. And keep your penknife there as well, to cut me in necessary lengths.'

'Certainly I will,' agreed Bobby. And he rolled the string into a neat ball and put it in his jacket pocket, together with the penknife which he had also been given on his birthday.

The first useful occasion arose during the very next afternoon, when Bobby was on his way home from school. He was carrying some books and they were quite heavy and bulky. The handle of his schoolbag had previously given trouble. Suddenly it broke and the books fell on the pavement.

'This is where I come in,' said a voice from inside his pocket. 'Cut off a piece of me to make a string handle.'

So that is what Bobby did and the string handle has done a splendid job ever since, without breaking once.

When he sent a thank-you letter to cousin Barbara he thought that he had better mention the string as well as the present so he added a postscript – *Did you know that the piece of string tied round the parcel which you sent me was magic?*

Barbara sent an immediate reply which was

rather abrupt, though she didn't mean it to be:

Dear Bobby,
    Don't be silly. How can string be magic?
                    Love from Barbara

  To which Bobby sent back a further letter, this time enclosing a piece cut from the magic string:

Dear Barbara,
    Wait and see. Always keep this piece of string in your pocket. Sooner or later it will prove how magic it is by talking to you and doing something useful.
                    Love from Bobby

  Well, there wasn't much that could be said in reply to that, was there? And as they had both spent precious pocket money by sending letters to and fro on the subject the correspondence ceased for a time.
  But not for long. Three weeks later there was an excited epistle from cousin Barbara:

Dear Bobby,
    I must apologise for doubting your word. That piece of string which you returned to me really *was* magic. I was leaving school

with my friends on a very windy afternoon last week when the frayed elastic which keeps my school hat on broke. It bounced along the road and I had to rush along chasing it with all my friends laughing at me. I was very annoyed, I can tell you, and when I caught my hat I was muttering furiously to myself when a voice from inside my blazer pocket said 'Keep your hair on! And use me to keep your hat over it!' The voice must have come from that piece of string because there was nothing else in my pocket. So I used the string instead of the elastic, and my hat has stayed on safely ever since, though the weather has been windier than ever. What is more, the dazzling white string looks far smarter than black elastic.

Love from Barbara

Well, that really *did* prove it, didn't it?

But magic number three was the most exciting and useful of all. Bobby felt very proud of himself because he had been selected to play for his school football team against another school one Saturday morning. He had changed into his smart blue-and-white striped football kit and was tying up the laces of his football boots when one of them broke. Oh dear, what was he to do?

As usual the magic string proved equal to the occasion. A voice came from the pocket of his blazer, which was hanging on a peg behind him, 'Use some of me. I will make an excellent lace and I'm the right colour too.'

So Bobby cut the exact length of string for his lace with his new penknife and, my word, did that prove to be more magic than ever?

It most certainly did. In the football match Bobby Brewster played brilliantly. Not only did

he score a goal with that boot in the first half, but in the second half he scored the winning goal – again with that boot laced with magic string.

And since then, wearing those boots with one magic lace (which has never broken though the real lace used in the other boot sometimes has), Bobby has developed into the best footballer in the whole school. He has scored at least one goal in every single match, always with the boot laced with magic string, of course.

Now Bobby still has a last piece of magic string, which he always keeps in his pocket. It is difficult to decide how it can possibly be magic because it is only a tiddly, short piece. But I am sure that it will find a way somehow. After all, however tiddly, it is still magic, isn't it?

And for the last piece of magic it will have to be something especially useful. What will it be, I wonder?

Your guess is as good as mine.

7　Old Ginger

Ginger was a tough old tom-cat who belonged to nobody but was loved by everybody. He was by no means handsome, with scruffy ginger fur, one ear, and a nose scarred in a fight with a dog which he had undoubtedly won. All the cats in the district loved Ginger, the lady cats because he was a bit of a lad with a twinkle in his eye who was always willing to play with their kittens, the gentleman cats because he was one of the lads who would go hunting with the best of them.

The Brewster family and all their neighbours loved Ginger because he was a real Old Soldier of a cat. When he was 'at home' he paid a regular round of visits to their houses at different times of the day. They all gave him something to eat and drink, but he arranged his proper dinner-time visit to a different home each day, so that he could scrounge a varied menu.

Then, after seeing all his friends, both human and catty, he returned for the night (when not out on the prowl) to a disused greenhouse. It was owned by a friend of the Brewsters – a lonely old gentleman who lived all by himself in a large house with a garden full of weeds. Every morning he left a good breakfast in the yard for Old Ginger to eat before the old cat set out on his rounds.

This routine was followed for some months and then, suddenly, Old Ginger would disappear for several weeks. He went walkabout, as they say in Australia about Aborigines who wander away from their homes for miles every now and then. How many miles Ginger wandered no one knew, but Bobby's father once thought that he saw him in a village several miles away. What made him wonder was that it was dinner-time and the ginger cat was eating a large meal from a plate in a back garden. So it very likely *was* Ginger!

Then, after a few weeks, Old Ginger would return home and the Brewsters would see him enter the garden. They would run outside crying, 'Here's Old Ginger back again.' He would purr loudly and turn over on his back so that they could rub his tummy, and they would give him a bowl of milk before he wandered away to visit their neighbours. Unless it was dinner-time – in which case a full two-course meal had to be provided.

And this regular round continued until the time for his next walkabout.

Years passed. Bobby Brewster, who was a baby when he first met Old Ginger, was nearly nine years old, and his mother and father had known him for years before that. Exactly how old Old Ginger was no one knew, but tinges of grey merged with the ginger fur on his face and he began to move less freely. Then he disappeared for some days and people said to each other, 'I wonder where Old Ginger is? Surely at his age he can't have gone for another of his walkabouts!'

He hadn't.

One afternoon Bobby saw the well-known ginger figure creep slowly through the garden hedge. He and his mother and father ran outside and dear Old Ginger staggered to greet them. He turned over on his back with difficulty for his usual tummy tickle and purred, but his purr was feeble. They gave him a bowl of milk but he only sipped at it and did not lap it up with his usual relish. Then he limped away with stiff joints to visit the neighbours.

On the following morning Bobby was passing
the house with the disused greenhouse in the
weedy garden. The old gentleman called him
over. 'I have some bad news for you, Bobby,' he
said. 'This morning Old Ginger had not touched
his breakfast. I went out to the greenhouse and
found him there, lying still. He had died peace-
fully during the night. I have buried him in the

garden.' A tear came into Bobby's eyes but then he thought, there's no need to feel sad. Old Ginger had a good life and made many many, many friends.

And there was no doubt about it. For those past few days Ginger had not gone walkabout. He had felt tired and unable to walk freely so after breakfast he had hidden himself away in the greenhouse. He knew that his end was near, but he had made one last supercatty effort to visit all those friends who he loved and who loved him. He had forced himself on his regular rounds to say goodbye before returning to his last resting place.

No one will ever forget Old Ginger, the Brewsters and their neighbours because he was a real Old Soldier of a cat and a loyal friend, tom-cats because he was one of the boys, and lady cats because he had a twinkle in his eye.

And to keep memories fresh, not only in the Brewster district but in his walkabout areas as well, there are plenty of little Gingers to remember him by.

There is a happy end to this story. Two of the little Gingers – a boy kitten called Marmaduke and a girl kitten called Enid, have adopted the lonely old gentleman who lives all by himself in the large house with a garden full of weeds. To say that he looks after them would not be entirely accurate because in many ways *they* look after *him*. But he certainly feeds them well, and in return they keep him company. Every night one or the other (and sometimes both) sleep on his bed. So he is now not quite such a lonely old gentleman, and he has two good reasons to be thankful to dear old Ginger.

8   *Listening is Fun*

There was once a boy who talked far too much.
By 'once' I don't mean that he was the only one.
Lots of people talk far too much, not only boys
but girls as well, and grown-ups of both sexes
even more so. But that particular boy happens to
be the hero of this story. Can you guess his
name? Bobby Brewster of course!

When he woke early in the morning he would
lie in bed reading – out loud! Throughout breakfast there was constant chatter, and Willy Watson, with whom he walked to school, could
never get a word in edgeways. As for school –
these remarks on some of his reports speak for
themselves.

'Bobby is a real chatterbox.'

'Bobby is a very talkative boy.'

And finally, in desperation, 'I *do* wish that

Bobby would stop talking sometimes!'

Now, when people talk all the time they leave no time to think, do they, so a lot of what they say is likely to be nonsense. The result was that some people thought that Bobby was rather a silly boy, although in fact he can be quite sensible when he tries. Then things happened which changed those people's bad opinions.

The first sign came one morning when Bobby woke up with the snuffles. They were not bad snuffles and his mother sent him to school with a supply of tissues. Then, after morning break, he started to sneeze. It is bad enough when children are always chattering in class, but sneezing is far worse, and by the time the bell went Mr Limcano, his teacher, could stand it no longer. He told Bobby to stay at home that afternoon if his cold was no better.

During dinner at home it was worse. He ate very little, looked flushed, and did nothing but sneeze.

'I'm going to take your temperature,' said Mrs Brewster.

She did – and it was 39°!

'Bed for you, my lad,' said his mother, and for once Bobby did not object because by then he did not feel at all well.

In bed he couldn't be bothered to read. He

tossed and turned all the afternoon, and that night he felt very hot and had silly dreams that made no sense but were worrying all the same. Then, when he woke the following morning, his throat felt extremely sore.

'How do you feel this morning, dear?' asked his mother brightly when she entered the bedroom to pull the curtains.

Bobby tried to reply but when he opened his mouth only a croak came out, so he pointed to his neck. His mother looked inside his mouth and said, 'Your throat is very sore and you have lost your voice.'

Well, that was obvious, wasn't it? And a funny way of putting it too. It sounded as if the missing voice might be found by searching in the bedclothes or under the bed! But Bobby could make no reply.

Dr Hopkins was sent for and he came during the morning. He asked Bobby to open his mouth and say 'A-a-a-h' while he shone one of those little torches inside, that doctors always carry in their bags. He had a good look inside Bobby's mouth and then announced, 'Your tonsils are swollen.'

Do you know what tonsils are? They are those wobbly things that you can see behind your tongue if you open your mouth wide enough and

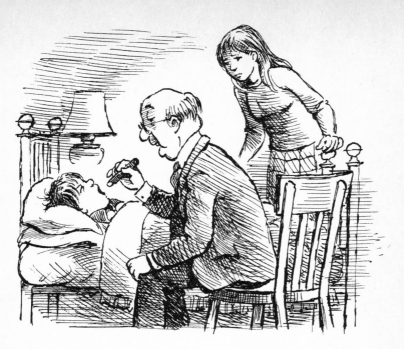

look right at the back. And swollen tonsils feel like footballs in your throat, so it was no wonder that Bobby did not feel well!

The doctor prescribed a throat spray, a gargle, and some pills.

But later that morning when Bobby tried to gargle he did not have enough voice to make the proper gug-gug-gug-gargling noise, and he had great difficulty in swallowing the pills.

During the morning he was lying listlessly in bed listening to the songs of the birds. And what beautiful songs they sang! He had never really noticed them before because he had been too busy talking. Listening was fun!

By afternoon he felt well enough to try reading a book. Without a voice he had to read to himself and it was more interesting than usual because he seemed to concentrate harder. Later, when he closed his book, he even enjoyed lying quietly and thinking about it.

In the evening his parents came into his bedroom to read to him and tell him stories, and once again Bobby found what fun it was just to listen. His throat was sprayed and he tried to gargle. This time there was just a little gu-gug-gug-gargling noise, and he managed to swallow a pill more easily before going to sleep. That night his dreams were pleasant and not all muddled like the night before.

By the morning his voice had started to return but it was still rather a croak and his mother told him not to use it too much. All morning he read that book again – quietly to himself – and it seemed more interesting than ever. By afternoon he felt well enough to get up and dress and go out into the garden. The songs of the birds were more tuneful than he had ever heard them before and he even heard little sounds from insects that he had never realised could make any noise. Listening really *was* fun!

By evening he looked and seemed so much better that his mother took him to the doctor's

surgery. Dr Hopkins congratulated him on making such a rapid recovery and said that he could
go to school on the following morning.

That night, when his parents went upstairs to
tuck him up, Bobby made a most surprising
remark. 'Do you know,' he said, 'it has been
lovely having no voice!'

Mr and Mrs Brewster looked at each other
with a single thought – Yes, and not only lovely
for you! – but they were sensible enough not to
say anything.

Bobby slept like a log that night without a
dream of any sort. He tucked into his breakfast in
the morning without a single word, and on the
way to school Willy Watson was delighted to do
most of the talking.

Mr Limcano's heart sank a little when he first saw Bobby sitting at his usual desk, but through-out class he did not once have to say, 'Stop talking!' And in the afternoon Bobby worked so hard and noiselessly that Mr Limcano began to have hopes.

His hopes must have been realised, too, for the remark on Bobby's report later that term read as follows: *Bobby has had a good term. He is far less talkative and far more sensible.*

So, you see, although that sore throat and those swollen tonsils had been uncomfortable at the time, in the end they proved to have been a blessing for all concerned!

9 *Fingerfaces*

At first Bobby Brewster was disappointed when he saw that his birthday present from Aunt Angela was a pair of knitted woollen gloves. Aunt Angela may be an expert knitter and woollen gloves may be useful for keeping hands warm in bitter weather, but they can hardly be described as exciting presents, can they?

But he soon changed his mind. He tried on his right glove to make sure that it was a good fit and found that Aunt Angela had cleverly knitted a face on the top of each finger. And one face, on the big middle finger, was so lifelike that he could not resist looking straight at it and saying, 'You are Fingerface Fred.'

Then a very funny thing happened. The face replied, 'I could have told you that!' It did, really.

'Was that you? Do you mean to tell me that

you can talk?' asked an astonished Bobby.

'Of course I can if you can hear me,' was the reply. 'Though I usually only talk to other fingerfaces and not to people. But when you seemed to think that I was silly enough not to know my own name, I simply had to speak out to you.'

'I do beg your pardon,' said Bobby. 'I had no idea.'

'But be sure to keep my talking to you a secret between ourselves,' urged Fingerface Fred.

'I certainly will,' agreed Bobby.

'Now let me introduce my family,' said Fred.

'Your family!' cried Bobby.

'Yes, they live with me on your right-hand glove – the Wright family, spelt with a WR,' explained Fred. 'First, on the thumb, my wife, fat Freda.'

'Isn't it rather rude to call her fat Freda?' asked Bobby.

'She doesn't mind – she likes being fat, don't you, Freda?' Fred asked his wife, who made no reply but smiled broadly. So she can't have objected.

'Next to me, on one side, is my big son Ferdinand, on my other side my daughter, Fiona, and on the little finger is tich Francis.'

'How do you do,' said Bobby, and they all

bowed politely, without saying anything.

'Our names all start with an F because we are fingerfaces,' explained Fred.

At that moment Bobby's mother called to him that breakfast was ready. Before going downstairs he neatly packed his presents.

'Don't forget,' said Fred, 'mum's the word.' Then Bobby folded his gloves together and put them in the top drawer of his chest of drawers. He would not be wearing them that day because it was not cold enough.

Then, at bedtime, he thought he would inspect the fingerfaces again and to his surprise, when he put his right glove on, Ferdinand was missing. Bobby asked Fred where he was.

'He has gone to visit his girlfriend,' Fred replied. 'Luckily there are only three in the family so there is room for him there. They live next door.'

'Where's next door?' asked Bobby.

'It varies,' answered Fred. 'When you are wearing your gloves it is separate, but when you fold us together it is semi-detached. Next door is your other glove, where the Leftey family live. Mrs Lilian Leftey, who is a widow, her pretty daughter Lucy, and Leslie, her small son.'

Bobby put on his left glove and yes, there they were, with Frederick Wright close to Lucy Leftey, who certainly was attractive.

Well, from then on Bobby Brewster had great fun with his fingerfaces. After his gloves had been folded together during the day he always put them on in the evening and found that there had been all sorts of comings and going between the Wright and Leftey families. One evening, when he wanted to look in at a football match on the television, all the males from both families had assembled on one glove to watch it with him. The ladies were together on the other glove, probably enjoying a good old gossip. On another night their roles were exchanged. Bobby wanted to watch *Coronation Street*, and there were the ladies on one glove waiting to watch it

with him, while the men probably talked football on the other.

The two little fingerface boys turned out to be
both clever and useful. Francis Wright was good
at sums and Leslie Leftey at handwriting. Luckily Bobby is ambidextrous. Do you know what
that means? It means that he can use both hands
well, even for writing. And when doing his
homework he found that if he wore his right
glove for sums they always came out right. (Or

should it be wright?) When wearing his left glove
his handwriting was so neat that he was even
given full marks for it – which was something
that had never happened before.

Another good thing came from having fingerfaces. In the past Bobby had an unfortunate habit

of chewing all the fingers of his woollen gloves. Without thinking he started chewing the tops of the fingerfaces, but Fred complained so bitterly on their behalf that he soon put a stop to that – much to the relief of Mrs Brewster who had grown tired of darning chewed holes in glove fingers.

There were occasional difficulties. Fred told Bobby that both families of fingerfaces thought it most unfair that he never wore his gloves on sunny days but only in bitter weather. Once, after a particularly cold day, they all caught nasty colds. Bobby spent a sleepless night in bed because of constant coughs and sneezes from his chest of drawers. After that he agreed to put them on sometimes on warm days and the children at school teased him and called him a cissy for wearing gloves during the summer. Once for a special treat he wore his gloves on a picnic, much to his mother's disgust. She called him a silly boy, which was most unfair because he was only trying to be kind to the fingerfaces. But he didn't say why. He had made a promise to Fingerface Fred.

Easily the most exciting event happened during the summer holidays when Bobby kept his gloves folded in his chest of drawers most of the time. Ferdinand Wright and Lucy Leftey were able to spend so much time together that they fell deeply in love and decided to get married. On the wedding day Bobby thought that he heard a peal of church bells coming from the drawer in his bedroom but that was probably his imagination. We all know that Bobby Brewster has a vivid imagination, don't we? But in the evening he certainly heard sounds of jollification, and on the following morning, when he slipped his gloves on, he found that Ferdinand and Lucy were both missing. I suppose that they must have gone away on their honeymoon. I wonder where?

On returning home in a fortnight the newly-weds, Mr and Mrs Wright, shared home with Mrs Linda Leftey, and now Bobby possesses a glove which is both Wright and Leftey at the same time!

I wonder if Ferdinand and Lucy will have a family? If so, the vacant thumb (on the Leftey glove) will be ideal for a chubby baby-face, won't it?

But I hope it won't cry at nights in Bobby's bedroom drawer and keep him awake!

10　*The Cuckoo-Clock*

Of all the pieces of furniture in the Brewster house, Bobby Brewster is fondest of the cuckoo-clock which hangs on the dining-room wall. This clock has a little platform in front and every quarter of an hour a tiny door opens and out pops a cuckoo. If the time is a quarter past the hour, the cuckoo says 'Cuckoo' and pops straight back into its house again. At half-past it cuckoos twice, at a quarter-to three times, and every hour it sings the longest song of all – 'Cuckoo-cuckoo-cuckoo-cuckoo' – and then home it goes.

Ever since Bobby Brewster can remember, he has been fascinated by this clock, and whenever he has friends to a party he asks Mr Brewster to show them how to wind it up. Mr Brewster pulls down a chain – up goes a weight – he waggles the pendulum, and then the clock goes for a whole day without stopping.

Anyway, I expect a lot of you know about cuckoo-clocks, because you have one at home – so I won't describe it any more. But, you see, Bobby Brewster's clock has a magic cuckoo in it. It has, really. Even Bobby himself didn't know this until, one day, a very funny thing happened.

Bobby was alone in the dining-room reading a book when the clock hands reached the hour.

'Cuckoo-cuckoo-cuckoo-cuckoo' sang the cuckoo, and Bobby looked up to watch it pop back through the door. But it didn't. It stayed out on the platform, looked straight at Bobby, and winked – a great big wink with the left eye.

Of course Bobby Brewster winked back.

'Hullo,' said the cuckoo.

'I beg your pardon,' said Bobby.

'I said, "Hullo",' repeated the cuckoo.

HULLO

'I didn't know you could talk,' said Bobby.

'You've never tried to talk to me before,' replied the cuckoo.

'I've never been given the chance,' protested Bobby. 'You're always in such a rush to pop back inside your clock that I've never seen your face, let alone watched you wink.'

'I'm very sorry,' said the cuckoo. 'Life is so hectic with cuckooing every quarter of an hour that I get easily confused.'

'Well, now you are here, what about staying outside and having a nice chat,' suggested Bobby.

'I can't do that, the clock will go wrong,' replied the cuckoo. 'But I'll tell you what, how about coming to have tea with me?'

'I would love to,' cried Bobby. 'But how could I get inside your clock? I'm much too big.'

'Leave that to me,' the cuckoo assured him. 'I can easily arrange it. I'm magic, you know.'

'Are you really?' said Bobby.

'Well, for one thing I can talk, which is magic enough for a start,' said the cuckoo.

'That's true,' agreed Bobby.

'What is more,' continued the cuckoo, 'I will arrange things so that you can come inside the clock and have tea with me. Just you wait and see what happens at a quarter past.'

80

And it winked, and popped back through the clock door.

Well, of course, Bobby Brewster was very excited. He simply couldn't go on reading his book, but he watched the hands of the clock go slowly round till, at a quarter past, the door opened and out popped the cuckoo again.

'Cuckoo,' it said, and winked at Bobby Brewster.

Bobby winked back.

'Billi–billi–billi–billi–bilo,' said the cuckoo, and before Bobby Brewster could ask it what on earth it meant, he felt himself getting smaller and smaller until he was no bigger than the cuckoo itself.

'Now jump,' said the cuckoo.

'What, right up there?' said Bobby Brewster.

'Yes,' said the cuckoo.

'I couldn't even reach you when I was a proper-sized boy,' said Bobby Brewster, 'so I'm sure I could never jump as high as that now.'

'Just you try,' said the cuckoo. So Bobby Brewster jumped, and, to his surprise, landed on the platform of the clock, next to the cuckoo.

'How do you do?' said the cuckoo. 'I'm very pleased to meet you' – and they shook hands.

The cuckoo opened the little door.

'Please go in,' it said. 'Tea is nearly ready. I'm

81

just waiting for the kettle to boil.'

Inside the clock it was really very nice. There was a lovely fire blazing in the grate, and the kettle stood on the hob.

Tea was laid on a clean white table-cloth, and everything seemed very snug and cosy.

'What a lovely room,' said Bobby Brewster.

'Yes, it is rather nice,' answered the cuckoo. 'I'm quite comfortable here in most ways. Of course, I have to be careful.'

'Careful, of what?' asked Bobby.

'The pendulum,' said the cuckoo. 'If I got in the way of that, it would knock me down,' and then Bobby noticed that all the time a great pendulum was swinging to and fro at the back of the room.

'Do you sleep on the sofa?' asked Bobby Brewster politely.

'Sleep?' said the cuckoo. 'I never have any time for sleeping. Excuse me –' and it rushed out of the door on to the platform.

'Cuckoo, cuckoo,' it then cried, and came inside again.

'I'm so sorry to interrupt,' said the cuckoo, 'but it was half past.'

'That's quite all right,' said Bobby Brewster, 'but did I understand you to say before you went outside that you never get time for sleeping?'

'Of course I don't,' said the cuckoo. 'I have to rush out on to that platform every quarter of an hour. I'm on duty here all day and night, you know.'

'Are you really?' asked Bobby Brewster.

'Yes,' replied the cuckoo. 'Haven't you ever heard me cuckooing in the middle of the night?'

'Now you mention it, I have,' said Bobby Brewster, 'but it never occurred to me before that it stopped you from going to bed.'

'Well, it does,' said the cuckoo, 'and I'm getting very tired of the whole thing. Come along now – we'd better start our tea. You take your time, but I must hurry. At a quarter to I've got to go out and cuckoo again.'

It was a lovely tea. There was bread and jam, cakes, and – best of all – sardines. Bobby Brewster was just settling down to his second sandwich when the cuckoo suddenly said: 'Excuse me,' gulped a sip of tea, rushed out on to the platform, shouted, 'Cuckoo–cuckoo–cuckoo,' and came back looking rather breathless.

'Phew,' said the cuckoo, 'I nearly forgot that time. I can't relax for a moment.'

'No, I can see you can't,' said Bobby Brewster. 'It must be very awkward.'

'It's ruining my digestion,' said the cuckoo, 'and I'm quickly becoming a bundle of nerves.'

The more they talked, the sorrier Bobby Brewster felt for the cuckoo. It had to watch the clock all the time, and whilst drinking a cup of tea it suddenly spluttered and rushed outside to cuckoo. There never seemed to be a moment's peace, especially as the longer he stayed in the room, the more Bobby seemed to notice the great pendulum swinging from side to side across the back wall. In the end he decided he couldn't stand it any longer.

'I really think I must be going now,' he said to the cuckoo.

'Must you?' said the disappointed cuckoo.

'Yes,' said Bobby Brewster, 'look at the time.'

'Good heavens,' said the cuckoo. 'I nearly forgot again,' and it rushed out, cried, 'Cuckoo-cuckoo-cuckoo-cuckoo,' and darted back.

'It was four o'clock,' the cuckoo explained, very red in the face.

'Now could you please arrange to make me a big boy again?' asked Bobby Brewster.

'Good gracious, I'd nearly fogotten that,' said the cuckoo. 'Let me see now, what is the magic word?'

'I don't know,' said Bobby Brewster. 'That's for you to say.'

'Yes, I know,' said the cuckoo, 'but I'm very sorry . . . I've forgotten it.'

'You've WHAT?' shouted Bobby Brewster.

'I've forgotten the magic word to make you big again,' said the cuckoo.

'What on earth am I going to do?' said Bobby. 'I can't stay in this clock all night. My mother and father will wonder where I am.'

'Well, you must give me time,' said the cuckoo. 'I'm so worried with all this work that I can't think straight. You just sit down while I try to remember.'

Do you think the cuckoo could remember that word? It kept on saying silly rhyming words like 'Willy-killy-nilly-tilly' and then shaking its head. Once it said: 'I've got it on the tip of my tongue,' but before it could think any more it had to rush out on the platform and cuckoo.

When it came back it said, 'No, it's no use. I can't possibly think properly when I have to keep rushing in and out like that.'

Then Bobby Brewster had an idea.

'I'll tell you what,' he said, 'you just lie down on the sofa and have a nice sleep.'

'I couldn't possibly do that,' said the cuckoo, 'I've got my job to think of.'

'Never mind about that,' said Bobby Brewster, 'I'll see to it.'

'You?' asked the cuckoo.

'Yes,' said Bobby Brewster. 'I can tell the time, and I promise that every quarter of an hour I will go out on your platform and do your cuckooing for you.'

At first the cuckoo didn't seem to like the idea.

'Now look here,' said Bobby Brewster, 'if you go on in this state, you'll forget the time and the clock will go wrong, and everybody will suffer. What you need is a good sleep.'

'Well, it would be rather nice,' said the cuckoo, yawning.

'Then just lie down on that sofa and leave it to me,' said Bobby Brewster. 'When you wake up you'll feel much better and you'll probably remember the magic word, and then we'll both be satisfied.'

'All right,' said the cuckoo, and it lay on the sofa and closed its eyes, and before you could say 'Jack Robinson' it was fast asleep.

Bobby Brewster watched the clock carefully. At half past he went out on the balcony and cried, 'Cuckoo-cuckoo.' At a quarter to he got a tickle

CUCKOO

in his throat and found difficulty in crying, 'Cuckoo-cough-cuckoo-cough-cuckoo.' It was a good thing the dining-room was empty. If anyone had looked up and seen, instead of the cuckoo, a boy in a blue jersey and corduroy trousers, what a shock they would have had!

Just before five o'clock the cuckoo suddenly opened its eyes and yawned.

'Well?' asked Bobby Brewster. 'How do you feel now?'

'I'm not nearly so tired, and my head's as clear as a bell,' said the cuckoo. 'I can even remember the magic word. It's . . .'

'No,' shouted Bobby, 'don't say it now, or I shall start getting big at once and break your clock to bits.'

'I hadn't thought of that,' said the cuckoo. 'You'd better go outside and jump on to the floor.'

'What, all that way?' said Bobby Brewster. 'I'll break my leg.'

'Oh, no, you won't,' said the cuckoo. 'Don't forget I'm a magic cuckoo. I can stop that.'

'Very well,' said Bobby Brewster. 'Thank you very much for the tea. I'll come again sometime and do your cuckooing, so you can have another sleep.'

'That will be lovely,' said the cuckoo.

Bobby Brewster said goodbye, went out on the platform and jumped. As soon as he landed on the floor, the cuckoo came out to say the magic word.

'Billi-billi-billi-billi-bingie,' it said, and winked. Then it added, 'Cuckoo-cuckoo-cuckoo-cuckoo,' and popped back through the door. Bobby Brewster found himself getting bigger and bigger, until he reached the right size. It was only just in time, for his mother came in the room afterwards to lay the tea, and, of course, she couldn't understand it when Bobby ate no sardine sandwiches. He had eaten five in the clock!

Since then, about once a week, when he is in the dining-room on his own, Bobby goes up into the clock to help that cuckoo. And from that day to this the clock has kept perfect time, and the cuckoo sounds so full of life when it comes out on the balcony to say, 'Cuckoo-cuckoo.'

11 *The Traffic-Lights*

Of all the people Bobby Brewster knows there is only one man he really dislikes. He doesn't feel guilty about it, either, because his mother and father dislike that man just as much as he does.

His name is Mr Bompass – and a very suitable surname it is because he manages to be both bumptious and pompous at the same time. Mrs Brewster says that all the local shop assistants loathe Mr Bompass because he is so demanding and rude. Mr Brewster says that up at the golf course Mr Bompass is notorious for boasting whenever he wins and swearing at his clubs for being useless when he is playing badly.

Once, some time ago, Mr Bompass called on the Brewsters for some reason or other, and when he noticed that there was a small putting-green on their back lawn he bragged to Bobby that he would teach him how to putt properly. But Bobby was in league with a toad who happened to be living in one of the holes, and whenever Mr Bompass tried to putt his ball into that particular hole Bobby coughed and the toad headed the ball out again! So Bobby won the match and Mr Bompass was so furious that he has never called on the Brewsters again – much to their relief.

But all this is old history, and this story has nothing to do with golf, though it has plenty to do with Mr Bompass.

Bobby Brewster's school is at the end of a drive leading out of a busy main road. For some time a kind lollipop lady tried to control traffic on that main road to allow groups of children – including Bobby – to cross over, to and from school. Most drivers waited patiently for the crocodile of children to pass but there were a few exceptions, amongst whom was – can you guess? – Mr Bompass. He tooted continuously and sometimes leaned out of his car window to shout abusive words. The great Bompass was in a hurry, so everyone must get out of the way.

The traffic increased so much that it became too much for the kind lollipop lady and, after a great deal of discussion with the county traffic department, traffic–lights were installed on either side of the road, complete with buttons to press and a striped pedestrian crossing painted on the road. The kind lollipop lady was still on duty, but her task was far less difficult with the help of the buttons and their traffic-lights.

There was one driver who hated the new traffic-lights, though. Need I mention his name? He sat purple-faced with fury, even when the lights were red with good reason, and if the kind lollipop lady was still guiding the last of the children across when the lights turned amber and green his fury knew no bounds. He was more abusive than ever.

Then, one afternoon when Bobby was returning home from school all by himself, there was
nearly an accident! Bobby pressed the button and
waited for the lights to turn red to allow him to
cross just as Mr Bompass approached, driving
far too fast. There was a screech of brakes as Mr
Bompass pulled up abruptly as the lights
changed. He leaned out of his car and screamed at
Bobby, '*You silly little boy!*' and a funny thing
happened.

Much to Bobby's surprise and the fury of Mr
Bompass, a voice – not his own – yelled back,
'*You rude old man!*'

Mr Bompass drove on, threatening to report
Bobby to his parents, his headmaster, the police,
the mayor and probably the Queen (but by then
he was out of earshot). When Bobby reached the
other side of the road the same voice, quieter this
time, said, 'Don't worry, Bobby. We will soon
cook Old Bompass's goose for him!'

'Who are you?' asked Bobby.

'We're the traffic-lights,' was the reply.

'You must be magic if you can talk as well as
show lights.'

'When we were installed we were just normal
traffic-lights to turn green, amber, and red as our
buttons were pressed,' said the lights. 'But Old
Bompass was so rude that we simply had to deal

with him. And in future it won't be by ordinary magic or even black magic, but worse. It will be by red magic. Just you wait and see.'

And red magic is exactly what it proved to be. It first happened on the following morning when the children – including Bobby – were going to school. The kind lollipop lady pressed the button to allow them to pass just as Mr Bompass drove up. The lights turned red and he drew up with the usual screech of brakes. A group of children crossed and was still being shepherded by the lollipop lady when the lights turned to amber. But this time, instead of turning green, they turned red again, and more children were able to cross. And it all happened yet again, with a purple-faced, furious Mr Bompass sitting in his car as children passed in front, laughing. Then when finally the last child had crossed, he was allowed to drive on, followed by shouts – not from the children or the kind lollipop lady, but from the traffic-lights – of, 'B-O-O-O-O, SERVE YOU RIGHT!'

This time Mr Bompass really *did* report the matter to the county traffic department. They sent a man to inspect the lights and then wrote back to him saying that they were perfectly normal and there was no cause for complaint.

But they were never normal for Mr Bompass

From then on, whenever he approached them in his car, even when there was no one there to press any button, those lights turned red and he had to stop. Then, as he sat waiting, there was the sound of mocking laughter!

The climax came when he could stand it no longer. One afternoon, when no one was about to press buttons, the lights turned red in front of Mr Bompass and he ignored them and drove on over them.

Did I say that *no* one was about? I was wrong. It so happened that Constable Wilkins was standing at the next corner, and he saw the offence and

his opportunity at the same time. He, like every
one else, had had trouble with Mr Bompass! S
he reported him for crossing red traffic-light
and in due course Mr Bompass was ordered t
appear before the court. In spite of his prot
estations the magistrate said sternly that cross
ing traffic-lights when they were red was a ver
serious offence, and he fined him fifty pounds!

That was the last straw for Mr Bompass. H
found himself a new job, sold up house an
home, and moved away to be rude to the unfor
tunate inhabitants of another town, to the grea
relief of – need I say? – the local shop assistants
the members of the golf club, the children at th
school, the kind lollipop lady, the Brewste
family, AND the traffic-lights, which have be
haved normally ever since and have neve
spoken another word.